# The People Paradox

# THE PEOPLE PARADOX

## Does the World Have Too Many or Too Few People?

STEVEN E. LANDSBURG

With a commentary by

STEPHEN DAVIES

Institute of
**Economic** Affairs

First published in Great Britain in 2022 by
The Institute of Economic Affairs
2 Lord North Street
Westminster
London SW1P 3LB
in association with London Publishing Partnership Ltd
www.londonpublishingpartnership.co.uk

The mission of the Institute of Economic Affairs is to improve understanding of the fundamental institutions of a free society by analysing and expounding the role of markets in solving economic and social problems.

A CIP catalogue record for this book is available from the British Library.

ISBN 978-0-255-36809-4

Many IEA publications are translated into languages other than English or are reprinted. Permission to translate or to reprint should be sought from the Director General at the address above.

Typeset in Kepler by T&T Productions Ltd
www.tandtproductions.com

Printed and bound by Hobbs the Printers Ltd

# CONTENTS

## ABOUT THE AUTHORS

### Stephen Davies

Steve Davies is Head of Education at the Institute of Economic Affairs in London. From 1979 until 2009 he was Senior Lecturer in the Department of History and Economic History at Manchester Metropolitan University. He has also been a Visiting Scholar at the Social Philosophy and Policy Center at Bowling Green State University in Bowling Green, Ohio, and a programme officer at the Institute for Humane Studies in Arlington, Virginia. A historian, he graduated from St Andrews University in Scotland in 1976 and gained his PhD from the same institution in 1984. He is the author of *Empiricism and History* (Palgrave Macmillan, 2003), *The Wealth Explosion: The Nature and Origins of Modernity* (Edward Everett Root, 2019) and of several articles and essays on topics including the private provision of public goods and the history of crime and criminal justice.

### Steven E. Landsburg

Steven Landsburg is a professor of economics at the University of Rochester and the author of *More Sex Is Safer Sex*, *The Armchair Economist*, *Fair Play*, *Can You Outsmart an Economist?*, *The Big Questions*, two textbooks on economics and over thirty journal articles in mathematics, economics, and philosophy. He's been hailed by Steven Levitt, co-author with Stephen Dubner of *Freakonomics*, as 'better than anyone else at making economics interesting to non-economists' and praised by political satirist and journalist P. J. O'Rourke for writing 'funny, jargon-free, shocking, and true essays on our material circumstances'. He inaugurated the popular 'Everyday Economics' column in *Slate* magazine and has written for *Forbes*, the *Wall Street Journal*, the *New York Times*, and other publications.

*This thought-provoking book is based on an IEA Hayek Memorial Lecture, given by Professor Landsburg at Church House, Westminster, London, in late 2017. While the lecture was not designed to create a formal piece of research, its content provides a considered and insightful contribution to the debate on world population.*

## FOREWORD

In the eighteenth century, English cleric, economist and demographer Thomas Malthus claimed that population growth was bound to outrun the food available and he argued that there should be limits on reproduction. Since then, many others have continued to claim that there are too many people in the world and not enough resources to support growing populations. A recent twist on the usual terms of the population debate occurred in 1980 when economist Julian Simon challenged biologist Paul Ehrlich to the now famous Simon–Ehrlich wager. Ehrlich's *The Population Bomb*, published in 1968, predicted famine and social upheaval if steps were not taken to reduce population growth (Webb 2020). After a long argument, Simon challenged Ehrlich to select five metals and a date in the future, betting that the price of the selected metals then would be lower than at the time of the wager, suggesting more availability rather than scarcity. Ehrlich selected five metals that he believed would be worth more in 1990 than in 1980, after adjusting for inflation. If, over ten years, prices rose, Simon would pay Ehrlich. If they fell, Ehrlich would pay Simon. In October 1990 Ehrlich mailed Simon a cheque, since the real price of the five-metal basket of commodities had fallen by 36 per cent (Pooley and Tupy 2020) even though the global population had increased.

In his Hayek Lecture, Steven Landsburg begins by telling us how people respond when asked: Does the world have too many people? Usually, the answer is a simple yes or no. He then asks: How do you know? To give an economist's perspective, he presents a thought experiment based on considering costs (negative externalities) and benefits (positive externalities). He concedes that there is obviously a physical limit to population, but this is different to the question of whether the world is currently overpopulated, or will ever be.

While Malthusians associate larger populations with negative externalities such as famine and assume there will be less of everything to share between humans, Professor Landsburg reminds us of the positive externalities that come with population growth. He cites Harvard economist Michael Kremer (1993), who suggests that the ratchet of human history over the last million years has been mostly upwards: 'More people, more ideas. More ideas, more prosperity. More prosperity, more people.'

Landsburg argues that we have not reached the point where the world is overpopulated. In fact, he believes that the real problem may well be that the incentives to have children are not strong enough.

In response, Dr Stephen Davies suggests that if we accept Landsburg's premise that the world needs more and not fewer people, this raises two questions for economists. Firstly, does having fewer people constitute a market failure that requires correction by government action? Secondly, should economists view people who do not have children as imposing costs or at least not contributing to greater general benefit? Davies also points out that many economic historians have argued that it was restrained population growth in western Europe that led to an economic revolution happening there, rather than in other parts of the world (Foreman-Peck 2009).

As an economic historian, Davies then asks the following question. If population growth does indeed lead to innovation and economic development, why did sustained innovation and development not really start until very recently? The answer Landsburg tentatively gives is the one put by Julian Simon, that until the 1750s global population had not reached a level high enough to support sustained innovation (Simon 2001). The quantity of the 'ultimate resource' had not reached a critical mass.

Davies also adds a warning that as societies become wealthier, they also become more akin to complex systems, which can be more brittle and prone to breakdown and failure. Even a small event can cascade to derail the entire system. Think of the release of Covid-19 from Wuhan, China, to the rest of the world. However, Landsburg would also ask us to think of a world where the people who developed the necessary vaccines had not been born.

Davies contends that since the early eighteenth century the world has faced three previous crises of complexity and systemic stagnation, but in each case the innovative process has burst through. He argues that we are currently in such a situation, and asks whether innovation will triumph again.

For Davies, the answer to Landsburg's question 'Is the world overpopulated?' depends on whether you think this fourth bottleneck of modernity will be overcome like the three previous ones. If not, the world is indeed overpopulated because the number of people has reached or gone well past a point of zero marginal return, i.e. the externalities of population growth and increased interaction will have become negative. If you are more optimistic and believe in the ingenuity of humankind to overcome such challenges, then Landsburg is right. Davies believes that we simply do not know whether the human species will succeed again.

Davies tempers his pessimism by citing Deirdre McCloskey, who argues that the cycle of progress has continued thanks to liberalism and individualism (McCloskey 2019; McCloskey and Carden 2020), which has broken through social limits to growth and weakened any attempts by the ruling classes to stop innovation where they feel it threatens the status quo. Both Landsburg and Davies contend that we need to sustain economic, political, cultural and social liberalism – and individualism – for progress to continue and for us not to stagnate.

Whatever your views, Landsburg's economic analysis and Davies's response as an economic historian help us to think about the many trade-offs to be considered in answering the question of whether the world is overpopulated or not.

SYED KAMALL

*Former Academic and Research Director at the Institute of Economic Affairs, and Professor of International Relations and Politics at St Mary's University, Twickenham*

May 2022

The views expressed in this book are, as in all IEA publications, those of the authors and not those of the Institute (which has no corporate view), its managing trustees, Academic Advisory Council members or senior staff.

## ACKNOWLEDGEMENTS

The Institute of Economic Affairs thanks CQS for its very generous sponsorship of the 2017 Hayek Memorial Lecture and of this publication.

# 1 DOES THE WORLD HAVE TOO MANY PEOPLE?

Steven E. Landsburg

Whenever I ask this question, there's always somebody in the audience who comes right back with, 'Well, of course. There's a limit to the number of people that the earth can support.'

That's someone who has contributed nothing to understanding the question because we all know that there's a limit to the number of people the earth can support, and so there is such a thing as 'too many people'. But that doesn't tell us anything about whether we currently have too many people. We could have too many. We could have too few. How do we decide whether we have too many or too few?

Let me start with some warm-up questions to think about whether we have too much or too little of some other things before we come back to the harder question of population.

For example, do I have too many socks or too few? Well, the answer to that is that I have exactly the right number, thank you very much. The reason I have exactly the right number is because I pay for my socks. I choose them. I decide how many to buy. Those decisions don't affect anybody else. I weigh the cost. I weigh the benefits and there's no reason anybody should second guess me.

Now, occasionally I make a mistake, and buy a pair of socks I end up not liking, or pass up a pair of socks I end up wishing I had bought. But there's no reason to think that anyone else could do a better job of filling my sock drawer. Given the information available to me, I'm buying the right number of socks. The key is that the choices I make affect me and no one else.

Is there too much pollution in the world? The right amount of pollution is not zero. If we tried to live in a world with zero pollution, it would be a world with no modern transportation, no buildings of any size and no way for me to get to London. There is a right amount of pollution and that right amount is not zero. Once you admit that the right amount is not zero, then you can ask, 'Do we have too much or too little?'

It's not immediately obvious. But I'm pretty sure we have too much. The reason I believe we have too much pollution is because the people who create the pollution – for example, the owners of factories – are not fully accounting for the costs they're imposing on other people. They feel some but not all of the costs. When you don't feel the costs you're imposing on other people, you tend to do too much of something.

Likewise, there are not enough people out picking up trash in the park because they don't feel all the benefits of what they're doing. Those benefits spill over onto other people. If you want to know whether the world has too much or too little of something, you've got to ask, 'What were the incentives facing the decision makers? Did they feel all the costs of their actions or did some of those costs spill over?' Likewise for the benefits.

When we talk about population, the relevant decision makers are the parents thinking about having a second, or a ninth, child, and the potential parents who are deciding whether to have their first child. What are the benefits and costs they are accounting for, and what are the benefits and costs that spill over onto other people?

I'll call the *private* benefits and costs the ones that the decision makers feel directly, the ones of which the parents are aware. These are in contrast with the spillover costs and benefits, which are the ones that affect other people.

Why divide it up in this way? Because the private costs are the ones we don't need to worry about. Parents are going to feel private benefits and costs in any case, just like me buying socks. As far as that goes, they're going to have the right number of children. It's only the spillover stuff that matters. I'm going to account for the private stuff only so that we remember not to count it in the stuff that really matters for this discussion.

What are the benefits of having a child? The big private benefit is love. People have children because they expect to love them and they expect to be loved back. That's huge. Another benefit, depending on the culture you're in, is that your children may be helpful on the farm or in some other family business. Maybe you count on them to care for you in your old age. Those are all benefits that people think about when they're deciding whether to have another child or not. Again, they feel all those benefits.

As for the costs, if you have a child, you're going to have to feed that child. You're going to have to clothe that child. You're going to be up late at night taking care of that child when he's sick. Later on, when they get a little older you might be bailing them out of jail or paying college fees.

Again, you account for all this when you decide whether or not you want to have a kid. You look forward to the good, and brace yourself for the bad. You weigh those benefits against those costs and that's how you decide whether to have a child.

But then there are the spillovers. Let's start by listing some spillover benefits.

**Trading partners.** Every child you bring into the world, every child that comes into the world, is a potential trading partner for other people. My children are your potential employers, your potential employees, your potential customers, you potential suppliers. I probably wasn't thinking of the benefits I was conferring on you when I was deciding how many children to have.

**Friendship.** Every time you have a child, every time I have a child, that child is going to make friends as they go through life and is going to enrich the lives of those friends. That's something that parents quite plausibly do not fully account for when they decide to have that child.

**Love.** Our children go out into the world. They love us but they love other people too. They greatly enrich the lives of those other people through that love.

**Diversity.** The more people there are in the world, the more diversity we have. If you like chamber music, if you like paragliding, if you like Ethiopian restaurants, if you like lectures at the Institute for Economic Affairs, then you ought to be glad that there's a very big population because these are niche pursuits that are hanging on by a thread, and that need a critical mass of people to keep them going. If there were half as many people, none of these things would exist. Diversity is a big spillover benefit of bringing more people into the world.

**Ideas.** This is the final spillover benefit I want to mention, and it's by far the biggest thing. Whenever someone has a child, that child is going to go through life having ideas. Small ideas like 'Hey, let's put on a play.' Big ideas like 'Hey, I wonder if we could make computer chips out of silicon?' Some of these ideas will benefit vast numbers of other people, not just directly but also because other people get inspired by those ideas. Other people get to copy those ideas, and get to improve on those ideas. If the child was never born, those ideas might never have been thought of.

Ted Baxter was the buffoonish newscaster on the Mary Tyler Moore sit-com. The character of Ted was played as a clown, and he used to say on the show that he was planning to have twelve children in the hope that one of them would grow up to figure out how to solve the world's population problem.

Ted was a lousy newscaster but he was a good economist. He had the right intuition. People come up with ideas.

Ideas solve problems. Solving problems leads to prosperity. Prosperity enables us to support more people, creating a virtuous circle.

Harvard economist Michael Kremer (1993) has a very striking paper where he looked at the last million years of human history and found that this is a cycle that repeats itself in all times and places. Sometimes, tragically, it gets broken, but he finds that this is a cycle that reverberates throughout history. More people, more ideas. More ideas, more prosperity. More prosperity, more people.

This happens for several reasons. The most obvious is that if you've got twice as many people, you've got twice as many geniuses. Bigger populations have better technology for the same reason that the biggest American high schools have the best football teams. But it's better than that.

You would actually expect twice as big a population to have *more* than twice the technological progress, for several reasons. First of all, unlike a high school quarterback who lasts for four years, ideas last forever. If you double the population in one generation, the additional ideas that come out of that generation stick around. They benefit not only that generation but every generation to come.

Another is that geniuses inspire each other. If you have four people playing off each other's ideas, you can get a lot more than twice what you get out of two people playing off each other's ideas. Now to be fair, that's not entirely true because geniuses also sometimes inhibit each other. Sometimes you decide it's not worth thinking about something because there's a smarter guy down the block who's going to beat you to it. This cuts both ways, though I think there's a lot of evidence that the inspiration side is the big one.

**The extent of the market.** Finally, a bigger population means a larger market, which inspires more effort to be inventive. So when there's a bigger population not only do we have more natural-born geniuses, we also have a lot more incentive for those of us with more ordinary talents to stretch those talents to the limit because there are so many people to sell our ideas to.

In fact, a team of economists at the Richmond Federal Reserve Bank has made an intriguing case for the proposition that the Industrial Revolution, and the tremendous culture of innovation that grew out of that, had to wait until the world population was large enough to reward large-scale inventiveness.

A big thing that happened at the start of the Industrial Revolution is that a very big idea started to spread – the idea that no matter what you did all week, it was worth occasionally taking off a few hours to think about how to do it better. That was a tremendous cultural change, which we take for granted. Taking time off from production, sacrificing a little bit of immediate income, in order to think about how to do things better in the future pays off only if you have a sufficiently large market. Arguably that's how the Industrial Revolution got its start.

Let me make concrete for you how much our lives have changed as a result of that culture of innovation.

There were modern humans around 100,000 years ago. For the next 99,800 years until the beginning of the Industrial Revolution, nearly everybody who ever lived did so at the subsistence level, the modern equivalent of maybe £400 a year.

There were times and places where it was better than that, but even people living on *double* that subsistence level still didn't have much of a standard of living. Very occasionally, a king, duke or prince would live a much better life, but often at the expense of others, who lived worse lives as a consequence.

In short, the odds are overwhelming that anyone living before the Industrial Revolution would have lived at the subsistence level, just like their parents and grandparents. just like their children and grandchildren.

Then some time around the year 1800 something happened. Incomes, at least in the West and starting in England, started to grow by about 0.5 per cent a year at a sustained rate. That was unprecedented. A couple of decades later, the same thing was happening around the world. Then by 1830, incomes were growing at 1.5 per cent a year.

Since 1960 – and this is all corrected for inflation – incomes both in England, the US and in fact around the world have been growing at about 2.3 per cent a year. This is a world average. It's also roughly an average for England and an average for the US. We are pretty average countries as far as growth rates go for the last 50 years, with incomes growing at 2.3 per cent a year.

What does that mean for the average family? Suppose you are a typical middle-class family living on a moderate income of, say, £40,000 a year. If that growth rate of 2.3 per cent continues, then 25 years from now your children will be earning £71,000 a year if they occupy that same middling rung on the economic ladder. And their children in another 25 years will be earning £126,000 a year. From £40,000 to £71,000 to £126,000 in two generations – that is the power of economic growth.

If you extend this growth for another 350 years, your descendants will be earning the inflation-adjusted equivalent of £1 million *per day*, unless they rise above mediocrity and live even better. And these are not future inflation-ravaged dollars but the equivalent in today's dollars. Now, you might find that wildly implausible and I certainly can't guarantee it's going to happen. But let me point out two things if you do find it implausible.

First of all, this is an extremely conservative extrapolation because I assumed we're going to level out at that 2.3 per cent growth rate per year that we're currently experiencing. In fact, the growth rate has done nothing but increase since it started out at 0.5 per cent 200 years ago. This is as conservative an extrapolation as you can make.

Second of all, if you find this implausible, try to imagine yourself 350 years ago with me standing here trying to explain to you what incomes were going to be like today. I guarantee you would have found that as implausible as you're finding this. Far from wondering where all that income was going to come from, you'd have been wondering where your next meal was coming from.

But where is all that income going to come from? Where does *any* of our income come from? Partly it comes from investment. Each generation earns income but does not consume all of that income. You don't spend all of your income on food, drink, clothing and entertainment. You invest some of it. When I say investment, I'm not talking about stocks and bonds. I'm talking about building factories and building machines.

Those factories and machines allow future generations to produce more and become richer. As we build a little more, then we have a little more income. And then we build a little more and have a little more income. But this cannot be the whole story. The reason it can't be the whole story is that factories and machines require maintenance. The more factories and machines you have, the more effort and the more resources you put into maintaining them. So it's more a case of levelling off than permanent growth, because so much of the additional income goes into maintaining this ever-increasing number of factories.

You can get some growth from this but you can't get permanent growth out of it. The only plausible way to get the kind of permanent growth that we have been seeing for centuries now is ideas. No economist has any other theory for where new income comes from. It comes from ideas.

When I say ideas, I don't just mean technological marvels. I don't just mean making computer chips out of silicon. I also mean the farmer who comes up with a new method of crop rotation or the business executive who comes up with a new method of inventory management. These ideas don't stand alone. They interact with each other and make each other more productive.

You can fly from here to Tokyo partly because some-body figured out how to build an airplane but also partly because somebody else figured out how to insure it. If either of those ideas were missing, you wouldn't be able to fly. You have a personal computer on your desk partly because somebody figured out how to make computer chips out of silicon but also partly because somebody else figured out how to finance start-up companies with junk bonds.

If you want to know which of those contributions was more important, a very rough guide is to follow the money. In the 1990s when the personal computer revolution was just getting underway, Microsoft's annual profits were about $600m. $600m was also the annual income of Michael Milken, the 'Junk Bond King'. By that measure, it looks like their contributions were roughly equally important.

It's not just our incomes that have grown thanks to the ideas of other people. It's also our leisure time. These are American numbers but I bet British numbers are very similar. A hundred years ago, the average work week was 65 hours. Today it's under 35 hours. A hundred years ago, only 6 per cent of workers took a vacation. Today it's effectively 100 per cent. A hundred years ago, 26 per cent of 65-year-old men were retired, and that was at a time when 65 was a lot older than it is now. Today 90 per cent of 65-year-old men are retired.

Child labour in 1910 was commonplace. Today it's practically unheard of in the West. So, we are working fewer hours per week. We are working fewer weeks per year and we are working fewer years per lifetime at both ends.

There is still a lot of child labour in Asia and Africa. A lot of people will tell you that that's driven by the predations of multinational corporations that somehow trick these people into making bad choices for their children, but this diagnosis runs up against the following fact. In England in 1840, the average English income was about equal to what it is today in those parts of Asia and Africa with significant child labour. The English in 1840 were sending their children to work at about the same rate that people are sending their children to work today in Asia and Africa. But they were doing it at a time when there was no such thing as a multinational corporation to force them to do it. They were doing it because sending your children to work is a natural response to poverty, which was as commonplace in England in 1840 as it is in some parts of the world today. It is a terrible choice between sending your children to work or sending them to bed hungry.

People make those choices. I don't think there's a good reason to second-guess those choices, especially because they have made the same choices around the world in different times and different places at the same income levels. As incomes began to rise in the West, there were certain threshold levels of income at which you saw large numbers of children getting pulled out of the labour force. In Asia and in Africa today we're seeing children getting pulled out of the labour force at about the same rates and at about the same threshold levels of income.

Economic progress – economic growth – has not just made us richer. It has given us a tremendous amount of freedom from work at every level including for our children.

In the early years of the twentieth century, the average housekeeper spent twelve hours a day on laundry, cooking, cleaning and sewing. Today it's about an hour and a half. A typical American housewife's laundry day in the year 1900 begins with her carrying water to the stove. She heats it. She brings the clothes to the big wash bin. She washes them by hand. She rings them out by hand, which is back-breaking labour. Then she goes on to the really oppressive task of ironing using the heavy flat irons that are continually heated over a hot stove.

The entire process to do one load of laundry takes her eight and a half hours and she walks over a mile in the process. We know this because the US government used to hire researchers to follow women around and count their every step as they did their household chores.

By 1940, our heroine has a washing machine. Her laundry day now takes two and a half hours. She walks 665 feet. Today, if you don't want to spend a single unnecessary hour doing your wash, you can buy a modern machine where you throw the wash in, you walk away and it messages you to let you know when it's done.

Most houses had no central heating, and no running water, and so routine household tasks included lugging seven tons of coal and 9,000 gallons of water around every year.

The average American worker since 1965 has gained 6 hours of leisure a week. That's over 300 extra hours of leisure a year, the equivalent of seven extra vacation weeks a year just since 1965 and all due to the economic growth that comes from the ideas that come from people.

It's not just income and leisure that have improved. I remember a time when I had a choice of three television channels broadcasting in black and white with no way to tape anything for later viewing. If you wanted to watch something that was broadcast on Thursday at 10 o'clock and you weren't home on Thursday at 10 o'clock, you were never going to see it.

I can also remember electric typewriters. Like many other mechanical devices, these improved with each generation until the last big innovation on the most advanced version was announced: the delete key. This was something brand new and exciting. You hit that key and it erased the last character you had typed. If you wanted to erase the character before that, there was no way to do it. And then electric typewriters disappeared completely.

My father suffered for years with pain and distress from a stomach ulcer that nagged at him every day. An ulcer that today is cured in two weeks with a pill. For the comforts and the luxuries we enjoy today, we can thank the people who invented video streaming. The people who invented cable television. The people who invented the personal computer. The doctors who discovered that ulcers are caused by bacteria. And we can thank the stroke of luck that prevented their parents from joining zero population growth.

If you think I'm cherry-picking, try this experiment. Get yourself a 50-year-old Sears catalogue. Correct the prices for inflation. Leaf through it and try to find one thing you would be willing to buy. It is almost impossible.

Or take a product like healthcare. For all of the problems with your healthcare system and with ours, healthcare today is a better bargain than it's ever been. I know that because if you ask any well-informed person whether you would rather have today's healthcare at today's prices or the healthcare of 1975 at 1975 prices, if that person knows anything about what healthcare can do today and what it could do then, that person will choose today's system with today's prices. Not to say we couldn't improve on it tremendously but it's still the best it's ever been.

The moral is that even the gigantic income gains of the last couple centuries vastly understate the improved quality of life. Henry VIII ruled an entire country and much more but I bet he would have traded half of it for modern plumbing, a lifetime supply of antibiotics and access to the Internet.

All of these things I've been talking about come from ideas. But it would be very dishonest of me to stop here. We can't talk about benefits without also talking about costs.

Politicians and journalists do this all the time. They try to prove something is good by listing the benefits or they try to prove something is bad by listing the costs. You can't do that. You've got to try and give an honest accounting of all the costs and all the benefits. What are the costs of population growth?

Before we discuss those costs, I want to mention one other big set of benefits that I'm not sure how to deal with. That is, if we have a bigger population, then a lot more people get to live. And that's pretty good for them. If they hadn't been born, they wouldn't have gotten to live. Presumably, they're grateful for being able to live. That's a benefit. Should we count it? That's more of a philosophical question. Do we owe anything to those potential future people? Should we care about these people who don't currently exist?

I think there are several good arguments both for and against that. If you're convinced by the 'for' arguments – that is, if you want to count those benefits to the unborn – then one way to think about it is to compare two different worlds. World A has 15 very happy people. World B has 30 people who are crowded and hungry, because somehow in World B none of the benefits of population size that I've been talking about has materialised.

How do you decide which of these worlds is better: World A, where everyone is very happy, or World B, where 15 extra people get the gift of life? One way to approach that problem is to survey the people in World B (or to forecast the outcome of a survey that you can't actually do, because World B doesn't exist yet). You offer them an option: 'If you like, I can randomly choose half of you, erase your existences, and the remaining half will then live much better. Do you want me to do that?'

If they say yes (or if I expect them to say yes), then I know that World B has too many people (or I expect that it does). If they say no, then I know that World B is actually *under*populated. Of course, this leaves the problem of forecasting what people in that world would actually say. We might be able to make some reasonable forecasts about that by looking at real-world data on the extent that people are willing to risk death in exchange for the promise of a better life.

For now, I'm going to stack the deck against increasing the population by not even counting this benefit. I'm only going to look at what's good for those of us who are already here.

We've talked about the benefits to existing people when population increases. Now let's talk about the costs. The big cost that everybody thinks about is resource consumption. One more person means one more person consuming land, consuming fish, consuming fuel. That means a little less for everybody else, doesn't it? Well, maybe.

If so, that's a spillover cost. But I think a lot of our resource consumption is actually something our parents accounted for and here's why: Where do you get your fuel? Where do you get your land? Where do you get your food? A lot of it you produce yourself. That's no cost to anybody. A lot of it you trade for. That's no cost to anybody. An awful lot of it comes directly or indirectly from your family. It comes from your parents who taught you skills over the years, and sent you to school. That's the source of many of the resources you've got. And not just the skills and the education but also the direct cash payments while they're alive and sometimes at the moment of their death.

Those resources come from whom? They come from your siblings. That's who would have gotten them if you hadn't been here. If you have an older brother, the day you were born was the worst day of that brother's life because you split the parental attention in half. You split the family resources in half. You split the inheritance in half. But your parents cared about your brother. Here's the key point. They cared about your brother and they still thought you were worth it. They thought you were so valuable that it was worth doing all that harm to your brother.

Well why should anybody second-guess them? As long as they cared about you, cared about him and cared about your other siblings, they were making the right choices just like I made the right choices when I chose my number of socks.

Insofar as your resources come from your family, I don't think we want to put those in the spillover category. Those are in the category that somebody accounted for. The decision maker – the person who decided you were worth bringing into the world – was aware of that cost. They were aware that it would affect somebody they loved and they still thought you were worth it.

A lot of people get this wrong. A lot of people have this idea that if I weren't here, there'd be a little more for each of the rest of you. That's not true. If I weren't here, there'd be a lot more for my two sisters, and nothing at all for the rest of you.

When we think about where a resource consumption goes, I'm inclined to largely put it in the private category. Not completely of course. Some of us steal things. Some of us go to war and steal things that way. Some of us become major polluters or contribute to pollution and that is taking from other people.

Arguably, accepting government assistance can be a cost imposed on other people, since you're getting your resources from other people. Those are all legitimate costs. If we ignore the private stuff, which is the bigger cost on the spillover side?

I don't know for sure how to measure these things, but I'll give you my guess. Most people don't become major thieves. Most people don't become major warriors. Most people don't become major polluters. So my guess would be that most children brought into this world bring far more benefits than costs.

Now again, I can't prove that, so I can't ask you to believe that for sure, but what I do want to ask you to believe for sure is that this is the only useful way to think about the problem. The only way you can ever know whether the world has too much or too little of something is to enumerate the costs and benefits. Take out the ones that were already accounted for by the decision makers, and compare what's left.

To sum this up, let's consider two families – call them the Hatfields and the McCoys – each with one acre of land. The Hatfields practice zero population growth. The McCoys double their family size each generation. After one generation, each McCoy is left with just half an acre of land. Then they double their family size again, and double again, and double again, until they're all living on tiny little plots. After several generations, the Hatfields have the pleasure of being rich and the McCoys have the pleasure of having lots of grandchildren. Each family got what it chose.

That by itself is not a social problem. That is an opportunity to celebrate diversity. Different people value different things, and that's perfectly okay. There is no social problem there unless these families start interacting with each other in ways that make their populations relevant.

If, for example, the McCoys decide to make war on the Hatfields, the Hatfields could reasonably say: 'You know, I think there are too many of those McCoys; I wish the population were smaller.' But if the McCoys provide markets for the Hatfields – if they become employers, employees, customers, suppliers, and above all if they start having ideas that the Hatfields can selectively copy – then the Hatfields could reasonably say: 'You know, I wish there were even more of those McCoys; it seems the population isn't big enough.' Unfortunately, the McCoys did not take account of the benefits their population growth conferred on the Hatfields when they were deciding how many children to have.

I have one child, a daughter. We stopped at one. That was a selfish choice. It was what we wanted to do. We weighed our private benefits and costs and that's where we wanted to stop. But somewhere in this world, and maybe in this room, is another young woman, maybe my daughter's age, whose life has been permanently impoverished by my failure to have the son who would someday have swept her off her feet. If I had cared as much about that other young woman as I care about my own daughter, I would definitely have had that son. But I didn't because I made the selfish choice.

Well, I understand selfishness. I do not understand encouraging other people to be selfish, which is the point largely of all the movements toward controlling population.

Finally, the last topic I want to discuss is overcrowding. It seems like there are a lot of people in the world. But you can fit the world's population five hundred times over in the Grand Canyon if you stack them right.

If you don't like that metaphor, take the country of France. Divide it into lots, which are the size of the average middle-class home in the US (a little bigger than the average middle-class home in the UK). On each of these lots put a family of four and you've just housed the entire world's population. Then you've got Belgium and Luxembourg for all the Pret A Mangers.

All overcrowding is voluntary. If you live in a crowded place, it's because you chose to live there. Often people say, 'Well, I lived in a crowded place because that's where the chamber music and the Ethiopian restaurants are.' But, of course, you need the crowds to have that stuff. If you dislike crowds more than you like the amenities that come with those crowds, then you don't have to live in a crowded place.

The world is nearly empty so to point to overcrowding as a cost of population, when all overcrowding is completely voluntary, strikes me as crazy. Given all this, why is there so much enthusiasm for population control?

A few decades ago, I was on a BBC documentary about population. My fellow guests were African healthcare professionals who were extremely disturbed by the efforts of the World Bank, the UN and other international aid organisations that were insisting on population control. These organisations, which used to provide antibiotics and bandages, were now supplying only condoms and IUDs. They were making population control a prerequisite to receive aid even though there were places where the population was not big enough to support schools and hospitals.

In those parts of Africa where the population has reached critical levels, there are schools and hospitals. You've also got a market big enough to support modern agricultural methods. In those places agricultural output has increased tenfold. People were trying to stop this. Why were they trying to stop it?

I think it's partly this fact about human psychology that when you're stuck in traffic on a hot summer night it's very easy to remember that the guy in front of you is imposing a cost. And somehow it's much harder to remember that the guy who invented car air-conditioning is conferring a very great benefit.

It is easy to remember that life would be a lot better if the person in front of you in the checkout line weren't there, and a little harder to remember that stranger who helped you change a tyre one night. The world is a lot better for the fact that that stranger was there. Londoners remember to complain about the crowds. They tend to forget that without the crowds, London would be Milton Keynes.

A world with more people is a world with more innovation, more prosperity, more friendship, more diversity, and a better chance of finding love. That's the kind of world we owe our children.

# 2 QUESTIONS AND DISCUSSION

DAVID BRAND: Julian Simon felt that even the size of the earth would not be a constraint ultimately because human ingenuity would invent space travel, so there would never be any limits. Could you comment on China's one-child policy?

STEVEN LANDSBURG: My inclination is that China's one-child policy was largely misguided. Of course, that was in a situation where you had terrible governmental and economic institutions which caused all kinds of spillover effects from population that you would not have had in a freer society, so it might have made more sense under the circumstances in China at that time.

Beyond that, I know no more about China's one-child policy than what I read in popular newspapers and magazines, so I don't feel qualified to comment beyond saying what my instincts are.

MARK LITTLEWOOD: Do you have any thoughts on whether the earth's capacity might not be enough?

STEVEN LANDSBURG: I don't see in the long run any reason there should be a limit on the earth's capacity at all. The immediate question is whether we've got too much or too little population given the capacity we've currently got. We don't need to worry about what the capacity is going to be a couple hundred years from now. My instinct is that I hope Julian Simon is right and I tend to believe he's probably right. I'm not sure with how much certainty I believe that but I don't see any reason in principle why humans could not grow beyond the earth, beyond the solar system, beyond the galaxy. Maybe that is the future.

Of course, there is the sobering fact that no other species anywhere else in the universe seems to have colonised the universe yet, so maybe there are some barriers, but that's very speculative.

CAILIN: I understand that you think population growth is beneficial, but do you not think that in the natural course of economic development population growth will cease?

At the moment, there are fewer countries in the first of the five stages of development, which essentially means that there are fewer and fewer countries which have women who are giving birth to multiple children. As a natural course of development, women start to give birth to two or three children. This number decreases because people invest in their children's education and so on.

Hans Rosling believes that population growth will stabilise at about 10 billion in 50 years' time. Is that likely, or do you think population growth will continue to increase?

STEVEN LANDSBURG: It is certainly true that the average family size is smaller now than it has been in the past. One thing that happened during the Industrial Revolution is people started shrinking their family sizes because, for the first time, it actually paid to educate your children. They wanted to conserve resources so they could afford to educate their children. Education did not pay off before the Industrial Revolution. It was a luxury and the financial return to it was negative.

That's all accounted for on the private side of things. If the optimal family size has gotten smaller, people will have smaller families as long as those benefits are concentrated within the family.

What will happen in the future? A lot depends on the future of the education industry. Is it going to be getting more and more expensive to educate your kids? Is it going to get cheaper as online education becomes more available? As we take more and more advantage of modern technology to make education more accessible and less expensive, as we improve the markets in education, as we get the government out of those markets, is education going to get cheaper or more expensive?

There's a lot of evidence that families are very responsive to these considerations when choosing their family sizes. Families are, incidentally, remarkably responsive to financial incentives at many times and in many places. We see in the data that when the financial incentive to have children changes, people change their family sizes very quickly. That's part of why I am so confident that on the private side people are making the right choices for themselves.

The Austrian government carried out a wonderful experiment twenty years ago where if you had a second child within two years of your first, you received a payment of around £15,000 from the government. Not a huge amount compared to the cost of raising a child, but as a result of the policy the rate of childbirth went up by 15 per cent.

Or was that just families having the second child a little sooner so that they got the benefit? No. If you look fifteen years later, the family sizes actually were bigger as a result of this.

What's going to happen to family sizes next year, or in ten years or a century from now? The answer is strongly tied to what the economic incentives will be, and we know so little about exactly what the economy will look like in the future. We *can* say with a lot of confidence that the economy is going to be better than the one we have now, although the specific costs related to childrearing remain very hard to predict.

ZACK MOSS: I'm from Forest School. You say that an overly populated country is better because there are more ideas, but given the housing crisis in the UK, do you think it's beneficial to have more people who are not able to get onto the property ladder?

STEVEN LANDSBURG: The housing crisis means that there are people who can't afford to buy housing, which is a private issue. Their parents are as aware of that as anyone could be at the time when they're deciding how many children to have. Presumably, if children are going to grow up and not be able to find a house to live in, families are going to account for that at the point when they're deciding how many children to have.

If you believe your children are going to live a miserable life, you have fewer children. Again, there is tremendous evidence across time and across space that families do make choices in that way. When their children are going to be productive, parents have more children. When children are going to live in poverty or live worse lives, parents have fewer children.

Parents can presumably accept that their kids are going to be miserable but still think it's better to be miserable, or that their kids are going to have trouble buying a house, but nevertheless think on balance that it's a good thing to bring them into the world.

If they're deciding that, I'm not sure why we should second-guess them. Sometimes they're going to be wrong because they don't foresee what the housing situation is going to be twenty years down the line. But nobody can foresee that better than they can. So again, there's no reason to second-guess them. Those considerations are already being accounted for. They're exactly the kinds of consideration that the rest of us don't have to worry about.

It's only when your choices spill over onto other people that there's a social problem.

JOHN DAWSON: Many people in the UK and in the US are fed up with the kind of population growth that results from immigration. They're unhappy about immigrants jumping the queue to get, for example, social housing.

But thinking about social mobility *within* a country, you mentioned that before the Industrial Revolution most people were living on the equivalent of £400 a year unless they were royalty or aristocracy. Does that mean that there was very little social mobility before the Industrial Revolution?

STEVEN LANDSBURG: Yes, at least if we equate or correlate social status with economic status. There was very little economic mobility because everybody was equally poor. Again, there were times and places where some people did a little better. But if almost everybody is living at the subsistence level, then almost everybody is living equally because those who are living below the subsistence level are not surviving. So, everybody was pretty much exactly equal at that time.

MARTIN COX: I'm from the John Locke Institute. I wonder if you might be overstating the benefits or understating the costs when you think about, for instance, the housing question. It may well be that when I have children I'm willing for them to have difficulty getting on the housing ladder. But if they live in a house which is going to be therefore more expensive for somebody else to outbid them to live in instead of them, is that not something we should think about?

The son that you never had who would have swept a girl off her feet, well lucky for the guy who got there a day later than he would have arrived because he could then sweep her off her feet.

You have said that when an author writes a book it's not as though no book would have been there in place of it. It would have been a slightly inferior book that would have had the market share that that slightly better book got.

STEVEN LANDSBURG: There are a couple of examples there, and I think the answers to them are different. On the first question with regard to housing, yes, we bring another kid into the world. He drives up the price of housing by entering the housing market. That's bad for everybody else who's looking to buy a house but it's good for everybody else who's looking to sell a house. Those benefits and costs wash out. I think that that's a case where I don't have much sympathy for your argument.

The other case is the son who would have swept a girl off her feet. He displaces somebody else who would have almost swept her off her feet. I'm not sympathetic to this case either because he displaces this person who then finds somebody else whom he likes a little bit less. That displaces somebody who finds somebody else whom he likes a little bit less.

Gender is obviously irrelevant here. But since we happened to start with a son, another son creates more competition on the male side of the market. At the same time, we're creating more choice on the female side of the market. I think the costs that we've imposed on those men are largely cancelled out by the benefits that we've conferred on the women by giving them more choice. You are right that the book market is different because, unlike the marriage market, one author can serve the entire market. It's not possible for one person to marry all of the women in the world but it is possible for one author to sell books to all the people in the world.

That's a different case because then you are displacing another author. If I write a book that everybody in the world buys, I'm going to get tremendous rewards for that. Yet I might have made those people's lives only slightly better because if they hadn't been reading my book they would have been reading Jamie's book and that's almost as good.

I hate to say this because I always like to tout the virtues of free markets but in free markets there are some people who are overcompensated. Among the people who are overcompensated primarily it's the people who are able in one fell swoop to serve an entire market. That includes book authors like me. Well, not like me but the ones who sell more books than I do.

SARAH COOPER: While the earth can accommodate many, many more people, how do you factor population density into your model? Although cities are great beacons of economic productivity, in other areas, for example, in Scotland you've got places where you've got great thriving industries such as oil but no one wants to live there. And then you've got other areas where people are hugely overcrowded. Can we provide incentives for people to move to those areas?

STEVEN LANDSBURG: Obviously, every part of the world has its own unique advantages and disadvantages, its own climate and its proximity to different resources. There are going to be all kinds of idiosyncratic reasons why one place is more or less desirable than another.

Overall, the big picture worldwide is that people are largely migrating from the less crowded areas to the more crowded areas. You see this in India where they're moving from the rural areas to Kolkata. Kolkata is very population dense but that's where people want to be.

In the US, we've got this small number of enormous cities. Then we've got this vast amount of unpopulated area and the net migration is from the unpopulated area to the populated area. The populated areas are certainly by and large – again, there are idiosyncratic differences – the more productive areas.

In fact, there's a recent very striking paper by a couple of extraordinarily good economists where they're trying to explain why productivity has slowed down over the last twenty years in the UK and the US. They argue that it is caused entirely by government interference with housing markets in the big cities, which is making it harder to find housing in the big cities, which is preventing people from moving to the big cities and confining them to places where they are less productive.

You can explain pretty much all the productivity slowdown as a result of people being forced to live in less productive areas, because housing is not being built in New York and San Francisco, because of government restrictions on how much housing you can build.

PAUL WITHRINGTON: The average number of children per household in Europe is about one and a half, which means in four generations we'll collapse by 70 per cent. This disastrous trend falls particularly on the able. Is there any way of reversing this trend other than calling for the Chinese policy being reversed with three per household aimed at the able in particular?

STEVEN LANDSBURG: If I am right that the benefits of extra children far outweigh the costs, then we want more children. Having 1.7 children per family is a recipe for disaster. What do you do about that? That's an argument for subsidising children, as the Austrian government once did. It's an argument for subsidising bigger families.

As a general rule, I am very sceptical of using taxes and subsidies to encourage good behaviour. Because as soon as you give somebody the power to tax and subsidise to encourage good behaviour, before long they're using that power to encourage bad behaviour or at least behaviour which is in their own interest.

I am very fortunate because the two things I care most about in public policy tend to dovetail. I care about prosperity and I care about liberty. For the most part, I believe that the policies that foster prosperity and the policies that foster liberty are the same policies. Occasionally, that's not true. That's when I get uncomfortable. This may be one of those cases where subsidising population growth is anti-liberty. It forcibly takes tax money from people in order to subsidise other people. But it may be pro prosperity, so it might be one of those cases where I have to have a sleepless night or two about where I come down on that.

# 3 HOW MANY PEOPLE IS TOO MANY? THE MALTHUSIAN VIEW OF HISTORY AND ITS IMPLICATIONS

Stephen Davies

In his lecture Steven Landsburg raises a question that has exercised many authors and particularly economists for over two hundred years. Is the world overpopulated or about to become so and, if so, how would we know? Concern over this question has been a part of economics ever since it was implicitly put by the Reverend Thomas Malthus in his *Essay on Population*, published first in 1799 (Pyle 1994). The question Steven Landsburg poses is the one that arises from Malthus's thought experiment: Can the world be said to be overpopulated, in the sense of having more people alive than is compatible with maximal human well-being? Malthus's initial gloomy conclusion was that not only was this possible, it was likely to be the default state of affairs with things such as the discovery of new lands bringing only limited and temporary relief. In the later editions of his work he allowed that it might be possible to restrain the growth of human population in ways that prevented that gloomy result and kept human population at a level that promoted a higher level of human welfare, through measures such as later marriage and sexual abstention (as opposed to the 'natural checks' of famine and pestilence). Much of the history of economic and social thought in the first half of the nineteenth century was a dialogue between Malthus and his followers and their critics (Mayhew 2014; Winch 2013). Early economists played a prominent part in this and the whole debate was one of the main influences on the developing discipline. This is the traditional debate that Landsburg is contributing to.

As he says, in terms of simple mathematics there is clearly a physical limit to the number of people that we can have on the planet at any given time. The question though is not about such gross physical limits but about what we may call economic and social limits. If having more people in the world brings benefits, is there a point at which the costs the extra people bring are greater than the benefits? If so, then at that point you could indeed say that the world was overpopulated. This though raises a second question. Granted such a state of affairs is possible, how would we know that we had reached or were in it? (There is the additional complication that it is perfectly possible for parts of the world to be overpopulated in this sense, even if the world as a whole is not.) All of this leads to the final question that the lecture addresses. Is the world overpopulated in this economic and social sense now?

The answer he gives is essentially the one set out by the late Julian Simon in a succession of works but above all his magnum opus *The Ultimate Resource* (Simon 1998). His thesis is that the ultimate resource of the title is not any natural substance, or even energy, but human beings and their ingenuity. That capacity, of ingenuity and inventiveness, is actually enhanced by there being more people, particularly if they live in relatively close proximity. That is for two reasons. Firstly, there is the simple fact that more people means more new ideas and an absolutely larger number of geniuses and highly creative people, even if they are only a small part of the overall distribution. The second point is more significant and is the one that Landsburg emphasises in the lecture. More people means more social and intellectual intercourse, more contacts between people, and more exchange and development of ideas through discussion, debate, imitation and amendment. This means that the production of new ideas and innovations (and hence of output of all kinds) will, as the population rises, go up by a higher factor than the increase in the population. It also means that you can get an increase in creativity and innovation with a movement from dispersed rural settlement to the higher density and closer proximity of urban living even if population is stable. One phenomenon that fits in with this analysis is the way that the populations of rural and thinly populated areas have lower recorded IQs than those of cities: it seems that being around lots of people stimulates the thinking apparatus and the more the merrier.

The implication of this argument, which Landsburg sets out, is that while overpopulation in the first absolute sense of lack of physical space remains a hypothetical possibility, the second sense of a level that has net negative effects on human well-being is vanishingly unlikely. Far from putting pressure on human society and resulting in a world where more people bring diminishing marginal product into the world so that the conditions of the population as a whole stagnate or even decline (the Malthusian vision), more people actually means more invention, more creativity and a greater and more rapid expansion of wealth and comfort. Crucially, the rate at which this happens is in excess of the rise of the costs that additional human beings bring and so having more people is a self-curing problem: the fact of more people, by itself, will lead to effects that mean that human well-being will increase. Surely though this cannot be correct? If it is, then it seems that there is no real limit to population growth, and far from worrying about higher populations we should welcome them and grow despondent at the prospect of stagnant or declining birth rates. More people actually means more production, at a higher rate than the costs of those extra people.

Obviously, there are some qualifications. If you extrapolate this indefinitely, then even before you reach the limit of physical space you might find that costs created by the growing population are now rising as fast as or faster than the benefits of more people. As we shall see, historically this was a serious scenario. The answer to the actual question Landsburg asks in his argument, however, is that we are well short of that point. In fact, as he explains, the real problem may well be that the incentives to have children are not strong enough, because the way the costs and benefits of having children are distributed creates an incentive not to have as many as would contribute to economic (and also cultural and intellectual) development through the effects of higher population. This is actually the main part of the lecture.

The starting point is the well-known economic phenomenon of externalities, which are benefits (positive externalities) or costs (negative ones) that accrue to bystanders who may be so numerous as to include the whole of society. The point he addresses is the question of whether having children creates a negative externality (similar to pollution) or a positive one. Given the answer to the first question, a secondary question follows. Are there too many children (and hence too much population growth), or too few, or about the right number? If children impose costs on the rest of the world as an externality by their coming into existence, then although the ideal number would not be zero (because of the costs of achieving that – the analogy is with pollution) it would still be low and possibly well below replacement level, if we conclude that the impact of the current level of world population is producing more harm than good.

This is currently a popular view and there are often popular pieces to the effect that, for people in wealthy countries at least, it is irresponsible to have more than one child – or any children at all – because doing so harms other people by way of pressure on resources and the environment (Timperley 2020). The central point of the lecture is to rebut this. The argument is that because more people correlate with more invention and creativity and more production, for the reasons given earlier, the actual reality is that we need more people not fewer. In other words, children create positive externalities via the innovation and growth-enhancing effects of population growth, and the likely conclusion is that people are not having enough of them.

Why is this so? The argument is that parents and maybe even children as well do not capture enough of the benefits that a growing population brings – in the language of economics they do not internalise those benefits. The costs, however, are internalised to a higher degree. In economic language, the positive results of a larger population take the form of an externality (a positive one) which means that the good in question (more people) will be underproduced relative to the welfare-maximising level. Conversely, the costs of not having children are also not fully internalised, because they are born by society at large, all the other people who do not get the benefits of a growing population, and by children themselves and other people who do not get to enjoy the benefits of associating with the other children who remain virtual rather than actual.

This all raises some interesting immediate responses. One is whether this constitutes a market failure that requires correction by government action. If the benefits of having more people are not sufficiently internalised by the people responsible for that (parents), then possibly the state, acting for society as a whole, should provide cash or other incentives to make this possible. As a matter of fact, there is a long history of such pro-natalist policies in many parts of the world, notably France (because of historic concern about France's low birth rate relative to Germany's). These have generally not been successful, at least not in the form of direct subsidy. What might be more effective would be more generally pro-family and pro-natalist measures, which would in theory work indirectly by reducing the perceived costs of having more children as well as increasing the perceived benefits. These have historically taken a number of forms, such as constructing the tax code to benefit parents who have more children and then stay at home to look after them, or, alternatively, providing state-subsidised childcare facilities for pre-school children (this has been followed in Sweden, where the birth rate has increased recently). The most significant have been structural interventions in the labour and housing markets to ensure that a household can be supported by just one income at the average level. (Because the cost of children declines steeply after the first two this has the effect of reducing the costs of having the third or fourth child.) Policies that favour the formation and stability of households would also have a positive effect on the birth rate (as well as being desirable for other reasons).

A second immediate response is that, on this argument, it is people who do not have children who are imposing costs or at least not contributing to greater general benefit. This suggests that the policies that Malthus himself advocated in the later editions of his essay, the so-called artificial checks on population growth such as sexual abstinence and later marriage (or indeed contraception, which Malthus did *not* advocate) are actually socially harmful. This is an interesting conclusion because many economic historians have argued that it was precisely the presence of such checks to population growth in historic Western society that were responsible for the modernisation take-off that Landsburg describes. In their view it was the restrained population growth of Western Europe that led to an economic revolution happening there, rather than in other parts of the world (Foreman-Peck 2009). For Landsburg this is, presumably, back to front.

The more fundamental response is that Landsburg has seen off one argument as to the world being overpopulated but not another, different one. The simple argument is that as population increases so too does pressure on the environment such as pollution or consumption of natural resources so that eventually these costs outweigh the benefits of more people and we have too many people. His response is that more people leads to more innovation which leads to improvements in the quality of life and also uses resources more efficiently so the benefits outweigh the costs, to the point that we actually have not enough people. However, history suggests a different response to his question. He himself notes that the take-off into innovation and sustained economic growth started around the middle of the eighteenth century. He also cites Michael Kremer and his description of a cycle of more people leading to more ideas leading to more prosperity (Kremer 1993). This though bears further investigation.

Kremer's argument, which Landsburg accepts, is that we can see a positive correlation between population size and growth and technological development for the whole of the last million years – the entire lifetime of the human species in fact. His findings are robust. However, they raise a set of questions about that relationship. The first is simple. If population growth leads to innovation and then economic development, then why did sustained innovation and development only really start very recently? The answer Landsburg tentatively gives is the one put by

Julian Simon, that until the 1750s global population had not reached a level that would be high enough to support sustained innovation (Simon 2001). The quantity of the 'ultimate resource' had not reached a critical mass.

This though leads to another more difficult question. If we look at the record, we can see a number of abortive 'false starts' in which a period of sustained innovation, population growth and economic growth takes place but is then cut short. Such episodes are typically followed by a regression to the historical norm with a decline in all three of these. We can see this if we think about some of the more notable such episodes. There was one in the two centuries after the death of Alexander, in the lands around the Eastern Mediterranean, another in the Roman Empire in the second century, others in fourth-century India during the Gupta era and in the Middle East between 775 and 861, under the Abbasids. China has seen several such episodes in its history, most notably under the Song dynasty but also under the Ming after 1550 and before the Song during the Han and the early Tang (Goldstone 2002). This could be explained by saying that they all petered out because there were not enough people in the world at that point to sustain it. The problem is that this is of course a circular and self-proving argument. We have to consider the alternative, that there was another check to the process of population growth and innovation which cut short all of these earlier ones but did not do so with the most recent one – or at least not yet.

One way of explaining the inability of these episodes to sustain themselves is by applying an adapted version of the argument made by Malthus. In this updated version it is not simple pressure on resources that causes episodes of innovation and growth to end (because that can be resolved via innovation) but other factors to do with the nature of knowledge and the costs and benefits of complexity. The first point is that, historically, human beings have reacted to the lack of growth and pressure of population and consumption on resources by developing a range of social norms, practices and institutions that work to share out risk in society, so that as far as possible any one person will not starve unless everyone does. These institutions are the 'moral economy' celebrated by authors such as James Scott and E. P. Thompson, and before them Karl Polanyi (Thompson 1971; Scott 1976). The problem is that while they provide security they also, by design in many cases, make innovation much more difficult and so create a situation where population growth can indeed have the dire results Malthus predicted rather than the beneficial ones Simon and Landsburg perceive.

Regularly, however, sheer human ingenuity and reproductive capacity break through this. Part of the breakthrough is the way that a naturally rising population leads inventive people to come up with innovative solutions to the challenges this throws up. This can then set in train a virtuous cycle in which more people means more ideas which mean more growth that can then sustain a larger population at an increased living standard so population increases again. This cycle of innovation and growth does not simply lead to more wealth and more people though. It also means ever-increasing social and economic complexity. As societies become wealthier, they also become more complex, in terms of the way they are organised and do things. Economically, this is because of the shift to more capital intensive or roundabout methods of production which produce more end product but take a more complicated route to get there. An example is the move from fishing by hand to fishing with a line and hook to using a rod, and finally to doing it with a specialised boat and equipment (Buechner 1989). The whole process now involves more stages and the cooperation through the market mechanism of a large number of people, which means far more human interactions and relations. This investment in complexity therefore brings benefits and many of the innovations that drive growth are ways of doing something in a more complex and roundabout way, with greater social cooperation.

However, this also comes with costs. More complex systems can be more brittle and prone to breakdown and in particular to systemic or cascade failure, where the failure of a small element leads to a cascade of failures that derail the entire system or process. Greater complexity also means in many cases higher coordination and transactions costs and it almost always means higher maintenance and replacement costs. The really big underlying factor though is that increased complexity means more acute knowledge problems. At all times human beings face severe problems of knowledge, as Hayek classically noted. Most of what human beings know is dispersed, dependent on particular circumstances, and tacit (incapable of being expressed or captured in words or numbers). Even worse, much of the information that would be needed for truly informed decisions simply does not exist at the point in time where a decision must be made because it will only move from the virtual and hypothetical into the actual as a result of choices made now – so it exists only in the radically unknowable future (Hayek 1948, 1967).

Hayek's other great point was that there are social institutions such as markets and language that enable us to deal with this challenge by generating signals that transmit the dispersed and tacit knowledge to observers. This seems to reinforce the point made by Landsburg about more people meaning more interactions, which means more signals being generated. However, that is over-optimistic. You can have too much in the way of signals: when that happens the 'noise to content ratio' goes in the wrong direction. Social institutions such as markets are better at dealing with large amounts of dispersed knowledge than either central planning or tradition (the often forgotten alternative) but if the number of signals created is too large, they too will break down and increasingly generate noise rather than meaning. So as population increases and societies become more complex, not only do the costs of that complexity increase so the benefits decline because of knowledge problems becoming more acute.

Another aspect of this is that innovation is not a straightforward linear process with the number of innovations an upward-sloping or even an exponential curve. Periods of innovation have historically not lasted. Instead, we have a pattern of what we may call 'punctuated equilibrium' in which there are episodes of fundamental breakthroughs and widespread experimentation and exploration, which are then followed by longer periods in which the 'gaps are filled in' with the new technologies put together in the first phase being matured. This in turn leads to a period of stagnation and increasingly marginal improvement, even while population is still rising. In the cases mentioned earlier what then happens is a retrogression, in which innovations and technologies are then forgotten or abandoned – as happened, for example, with much Roman technology such as concrete or advanced optics and batteries in the Arab case. The process appears to reflect the increasing difficulty in innovation after a while absent a paradigm shift or change in the frame of reference within which creators and inventors work.

This historical pattern and its connection with complexity was theorised by Joseph Tainter in his landmark work *The Collapse of Complex Societies*, first published in 1988 (Tainter 1990). Tainter's thesis is different from the more commonplace Malthusianism found in works such as Jared Diamond's *Collapse*, which see human population as the problem and its demands outstripping the carrying capacity of the resource base (Diamond 2011). The rejoinder to that position is the one Landsburg makes, that the carrying capacity can be raised by innovation and that, paradoxically, having more people actually does this by (given other factors) leading to sustained innovation. For Tainter the problem is that the innovative and developmental process is by its nature self-limiting because its very success leads to increasing problems and diminishing returns to complexity and specialisation. This means that eventually the gains from increasing population and consequent human interaction turn negative. At this point there is an episode of simplification or societal collapse, in which the complex systems and institutions break down or are actually dismantled. This is marked by such phenomena as the breakdown of complex and large-scale political systems such as empires and a similar reduction in economic complexity with a decline in the division of labour and the complexity of networks and relations. Most strikingly, there is a decline in population and a process of de-urbanisation.

It is important to emphasise that the term 'collapse' is misleading because of the association of that term in English with something sudden and abrupt or apocalyptic. In reality, simplification episodes last for at least 80–90 years and often as long as 150 years or more – so the process of simplification is gradual (Greer 2008). It is also catabolic, meaning that it can come to a halt at any one of a number of points, depending on particular circumstances. In the ancient world the process often did not stop until there had been a complete reversion to a pre-civilised state (as happened later with the Classical Mayan collapse) but from the age of Late Antiquity onwards the simplification process tends to result in a falling back by the measures of complexity and subsequent stagnation for a while rather than a complete regression.

This is what we observe on investigation in the termination of episodes of population growth and innovation or flowering, in many times and parts of the world, before the advent of modernity that Landsburg discusses. This pattern means that looked at in the long term the story of human living standards and of global population is one of stability or very slow and gradual growth even though there are many peaks and surges – these are counterbalanced by the subsequent troughs or stagnation. To return to our original question, why is this time different? It is different for two reasons: it has lasted longer and the degree of population growth, economic growth and innovation have all been unprecedented. The Simon explanation is that this was a matter of global population reaching a critical threshold but that has the problems of firstly being un-disprovable (and so not testable) and secondly not taking account of the arguments about the self-limiting qualities of complex systems, even spontaneous ones. Another is to emphasise the role of cultural or ideological shifts, which is the position taken by McCloskey (2010, 2016). The third emphasises the role of one critical resource, not in this case population, but usable energy (Wrigley 1983). In this model as well as increased complexity, rising population runs up against limits on the amount of energy available to do work and crucially to maintain the capital stock (Ophuls 1997). The modern world in this view has had the windfall benefit of access to unusually concentrated and compact energy sources in the shape of fossil fuels and that has enabled us to resolve the challenges of increased complexity by simply using more energy per capita – the question, of course, if this is true, is whether this can continue.

The other feature of the modern world is that the cycle of growth and innovation has gone through repeated in-stantiations rather than just one. Since the first half of the eighteenth century, the world has gone through not one cycle of innovation, but four – and we are in the fourth right now.

The first of these, which germinated in the later seventeenth and early eighteenth century and then rolled out after 1750, centred around improvements in agriculture, the use of water power to drive increasingly complex machinery, and breakthroughs in transport associated with better roads and canals. This Rococo economy was in many ways a perfection of the traditional technologies and economic organisation and was similar to the previous surges described earlier (the level of economic and technological development in western Europe around 1750 was roughly the same as that in Song China or Antonine Rome). The second, which marked a novel break through Malthusian constraints, began after 1750 but was realised in the period between roughly the 1820s and the 1880s. The central elements were the use of coal, steam power, railways and iron-hulled ships, the telegraph, and mechanisation. The third, which again began while the second was being realised but came to fruition after a crisis in the later nineteenth century, was the one that brought about the really big increases in productivity and created the world that we are all familiar with. The central features here were things like the use of oil and its products, the widespread use of electricity, synthetic materials (including fertilisers), the internal combustion engine, and mass production. The fourth is the one that we have been living through since the 1960s (although again many of the key breakthroughs or inventions happened in the twenty or so years before then). This time the main technologies and innovations have been in computing and information technology and communications technology. This one has had noticeably less impact on productivity than the previous two. If there is to be a fifth it is expected to be in the areas of GRIN (genetics, robotics/AI, information and nanotechnology but there will also have to be one in energy, which would make it GRINE).

In other words, there have been three episodes where the modern world has faced a crisis of complexity and systemic stagnation, a Malthusian barrier if you will but in each case the innovative process has burst through it. We are currently in such a situation, by various indicators, so the question is whether this will happen again over the next two decades or so. If we do, the benign process described will continue, if not then the modern world will prove to be merely the longest episode of growth and innovation and we will revert to the long-term norm. (This will not mean going back to the pre-modern world, for various reasons, but it would mean the end of many of the features of modernity which most people find welcome.) So, the answer to the question 'Is the world overpopulated?' depends on whether you think this fourth bottleneck of modernity will be overcome like the three previous ones. If not, then the world is indeed overpopulated because the number of people has reached or gone well past a point of zero marginal return – the externalities of population growth and increased interaction will have become negative. If you are more optimistic, then Landsburg's argument still applies. The problem is we do not know whether the human species will succeed again.

We do have one reason perhaps to lean to optimism. As McCloskey has argued, the reason why the cycle has continued is ultimately down to a particular approach to economic, political and social organisation – in two words, liberalism and individualism (McCloskey 2019; McCloskey and Carden 2020)). This is what has undermined the social limits to growth of all kinds and innovation and also weakened the other great factor, predation by ruling classes and deliberate action on their part to freeze the status quo and stop innovation (because it threatens their position). It is liberalism and individualism, economic, political, cultural and social that we must sustain if we are to keep the threat of stagnation and simplification at bay again.

# REFERENCES

Buechner, M. N. (1989) Roundaboutness and productivity in Bohm-Bawerk. *Southern Economic Journal* 56(2): 499–510.

Diamond, J. (2011) *Collapse: How Societies Choose to Fail or Survive*. London: Penguin.

Foreman-Peck, J. (2009) The western European marriage pattern and economic development. Cardiff Economics Working Papers.

Goldstone, J. A. (2002) Efflorescences and economic growth in world history: rethinking the 'Rise of the West' and the Industrial Revolution. *Journal of World History* 13(2): 323–89.

Greer, J. M. (2008) *The Long Descent: A User's Guide to the End of the Industrial Age*. New Society Publishers.

Hayek, F. A. (1948) The uses of knowledge in society. In *Individualism and Economic Order*, ch. 4, pp. 77–91. London: Routledge & Kegan Paul.

Hayek, F. A. (1967) The theory of complex phenomena. In *Studies in Philosophy, Politics and Economics*, ch. 2, pp. 22–42. London: Routledge & Kegan Paul

Kremer, M. (1993) Population growth and technological change: one million BC to 1990. *Quarterly Journal of Economics* 108(3): 681–716.

Mayhew, R. J. (2014) *Malthus: The Life and Legacies of an Untimely Prophet*. Cambridge, MA: Harvard University Press.

McCloskey, D. (2010) *Bourgeois Dignity: Why Economics Can't Explain the Modern World.* University of Chicago Press.

McCloskey, D. (2016) *Bourgeois Equality: How Ideas, Not Capital or Institutions, Enriched the World.* University of Chicago Press.

McCloskey, D. (2019) *Why Liberalism Works: How True Liberal Values Produce a Freer, More Equal, Prosperous World for All.* New Haven, CT: Yale University Press.

McCloskey, D. and Carden, A. (2020) *Leave Me Alone and I'll Make You Rich: How the Bourgeois Deal Enriched the World.* University of Chicago Press.

Ophuls, W. (1997) *Requiem for Modern Politics: The Tragedy of the Enlightenment and the Challenge of the New Millenium.* Boulder, CO: Westview Press.

Pooley, G. and Tupy, M. (2020) Luck or insight? The Simon–Ehrlich bet re-examined. *Economic Affairs* 40(2): 277–80.

Pyle, A. (ed.) (1994) *Population: Contemporary Responses to Thomas Malthus.* Bristol: Thoemmes.

Scott, J. C. (1976) *The Moral Economy of the Peasant: Rebellion and Subsistence in South-East Asia.* New Haven, CT: Yale University Press.

Simon, J. L. (1998) *The Ultimate Resource 2.* Princeton University Press.

Simon, J. L. (2001) *The Great Breakthrough and Its Cause.* Anne Arbor, MI: Michigan University Press.

Tainter, J. (1990) *The Collapse of Complex Societies.* Cambridge University Press.

Thompson, E. (1971) The moral economy of the English crowd in the eighteenth century. *Past and Present* 50: 73–136.

Timperley, J. (2020) Human overpopulation: can having fewer children really make a difference? *BBC Science Focus*, 21 January 2020.

Webb, R. (2020) Paul Ehrlich: there are too many super-consumers on the planet. *New Scientist*, 11 November (https://www.newscientist.com/article/2232011-paul-ehrlich-there-are-too-many-super-consumers-on-the-planet/#ixzz6yXleHdvd).

Winch, D. (2013) *Malthus: A Very Short Introduction.* Oxford University Press.

Wrigley, E. A. (1983) The growth of population in eighteenth century England: a conundrum resolved. *Past and Present* 98: 121–50.

## ABOUT THE IEA

The Institute is a research and educational charity (No. CC 235 351), limited by guarantee. Its mission is to improve understanding of the fundamental institutions of a free society by analysing and expounding the role of markets in solving economic and social problems.

The IEA achieves its mission by:

- a high-quality publishing programme
- conferences, seminars, lectures and other events
- outreach to school and college students
- brokering media introductions and appearances

The IEA, which was established in 1955 by the late Sir Antony Fisher, is an educational charity, not a political organisation. It is independent of any political party or group and does not carry on activities intended to affect support for any political party or candidate in any election or referendum, or at any other time. It is financed by sales of publications, conference fees and voluntary donations.

In addition to its main series of publications, the IEA also publishes (jointly with the University of Buckingham), *Economic Affairs*.

The IEA is aided in its work by a distinguished international Academic Advisory Council and an eminent panel of Honorary Fellows. Together with other academics, they review prospective IEA publications, their comments being passed on anonymously to authors. All IEA papers are therefore subject to the same rigorous independent refereeing process as used by leading academic journals.

IEA publications enjoy widespread classroom use and course adoptions in schools and universities. They are also sold throughout the world and often translated/reprinted.

Since 1974 the IEA has helped to create a worldwide network of 100 similar institutions in over 70 countries. They are all independent but share the IEA's mission.

Views expressed in the IEA's publications are those of the authors, not those of the Institute (which has no corporate view), its Managing Trustees, Academic Advisory Council members or senior staff.

Members of the Institute's Academic Advisory Council, Honorary Fellows, Trustees and Staff are listed on the following page.

The Institute gratefully acknowledges financial support for its publications programme and other work from a generous benefaction by the late Professor Ronald Coase.

Other books recently published by the IEA include:

*Sea Change: How Markets and Property Rights Could Transform the Fishing Industry*
Edited by Richard Wellings
Readings in Political Economy 7; ISBN 978-0-255-36740-0; £10.00

*Working to Rule: The Damaging Economics of UK Employment Regulation*
J. R. Shackleton
Hobart Paperback 186; ISBN 978-0-255-36743-1; £15.00

*Education, War and Peace: The Surprising Success of Private Schools in War-Torn Countries*
James Tooley and David Longfield
ISBN 978-0-255-36746-2; £10.00

*Killjoys: A Critique of Paternalism*
Christopher Snowdon
ISBN 978-0-255-36749-3; £12.50

*Financial Stability without Central Banks*
George Selgin, Kevin Dowd and Mathieu Bédard
ISBN 978-0-255-36752-3; £10.00

*Against the Grain: Insights from an Economic Contrarian*
Paul Ormerod
ISBN 978-0-255-36755-4; £15.00

*Ayn Rand: An Introduction*
Eamonn Butler
ISBN 978-0-255-36764-6; £12.50

*Capitalism: An Introduction*
Eamonn Butler
ISBN 978-0-255-36758-5; £12.50

*Opting Out: Conscience and Cooperation in a Pluralistic Society*
David S. Oderberg
ISBN 978-0-255-36761-5; £12.50

*Getting the Measure of Money: A Critical Assessment of UK Monetary Indicators*
Anthony J. Evans
ISBN 978-0-255-36767-7; £12.50

*Socialism: The Failed Idea That Never Dies*
Kristian Niemietz
ISBN 978-0-255-36770-7; £17.50

*Top Dogs and Fat Cats: The Debate on High Pay*
Edited by J. R. Shackleton
ISBN 978-0-255-36773-8; £15.00

*School Choice around the World ... And the Lessons We Can Learn*
Edited by Pauline Dixon and Steve Humble
ISBN 978-0-255-36779-0; £15.00

*School of Thought: 101 Great Liberal Thinkers*
Eamonn Butler
ISBN 978-0-255-36776-9; £12.50

*Raising the Roof: How to Solve the United Kingdom's Housing Crisis*
Edited by Jacob Rees-Mogg and Radomir Tylecote
ISBN 978-0-255-36782-0; £12.50

*How Many Light Bulbs Does It Take to Change the World?*
Matt Ridley and Stephen Davies
ISBN 978-0-255-36785-1; £10.00

*The Henry Fords of Healthcare ... Lessons the West Can Learn from the East*
Nima Sanandaji
ISBN 978-0-255-36788-2; £10.00

*An Introduction to Entrepreneurship*
Eamonn Butler
ISBN 978-0-255-36794-3; £12.50

*An Introduction to Democracy*
Eamonn Butler
ISBN 978-0-255-36797-4; £12.50

*Having Your Say: Threats to Free Speech in the 21st Century*
Edited by J. R. Shackleton
ISBN 978-0-255-36800-1; £17.50

*The Sharing Economy: Its Pitfalls and Promises*
Michael C. Munger
ISBN 978-0-255-36791-2; £12.50

*An Introduction to Trade and Globalisation*
Eamonn Butler
ISBN 978-0-255-36803-2; £12.50

*Why Free Speech Matters*
Jamie Whyte
ISBN 978-0-255-36806-3; £10.00

## Other IEA publications

Comprehensive information on other publications and the wider work of the IEA can be found at www.iea.org.uk. To order any publication please see below.

## Personal customers

Orders from personal customers should be directed to the IEA:

IEA
2 Lord North Street
FREEPOST LON10168
London SW1P 3YZ
Tel: 020 7799 8911, Fax: 020 7799 2137
Email: sales@iea.org.uk

## Trade customers

All orders from the book trade should be directed to the IEA's distributor:

NBN International (IEA Orders)
Orders Dept.
NBN International
10 Thornbury Road
Plymouth PL6 7PP
Tel: 01752 202301, Fax: 01752 202333
Email: orders@nbninternational.com

## IEA subscriptions

The IEA also offers a subscription service to its publications. For a single annual payment (currently £42.00 in the UK), subscribers receive every monograph the IEA publishes. For more information please contact:

Subscriptions
IEA
2 Lord North Street
FREEPOST LON10168
London SW1P 3YZ
Tel: 020 7799 8911, Fax: 020 7799 2137
Email: accounts@iea.org.uk